Franklin Street, 1957

Franklin Street, 1957

Poems by

John Ziegler

© 2026 John Ziegler. All rights reserved.
This material may not be reproduced in any form, published,
reprinted, recorded, performed, broadcast,
rewritten or redistributed without
the explicit permission of John Ziegler.
All such actions are strictly prohibited by law.

Cover design by Shay Culligan
Cover image *Radio Ball* by Jared Hankins
Author photo by Robert Fredd

ISBN: 979-8-90146-805-0

Kelsay Books
502 South 1040 East, A-119
American Fork, Utah 84003
Kelsaybooks.com

*My thanks to our Poetry Writers Group—
Sarah Russell, Steve Deutsch, Lisa McMonagle,
Teresa Stouffer, Mark Shirey—
the fierce, caring editors that help bring
my thoughts and words into clarity
and urge me to kill my darlings.*

Acknowledgments

Thank you to the following publications, where versions of these poems previously appeared:

Academy of Heart and Mind: "Fox Robe," "Luther's Story," "Lydia's Sampler," "The Cellar"

Ariel Chart: "Haircut," "My Dreams are Strong"

Literary Yard: "Alice," "Foot Race," "Mulberries," "Sister Loretta," "The Black Strap," "Uncle Ernest"

Lothlorien Poetry Journal: "In Prayers," "Old Photos"

Red Eft: "Charles and Lydia"

Rusty Truck: "At Age 5," "Cemetery at Towamensin," "Croup," "Fourth of July," "Old Photos," "Paper Route," "West Park," "Witch"

Contents

I. The Kid

Franklin Street, 1957	15
At Age 5	17
Glass Button	19
Funeral	20
Sleep Ritual	22
The Cellar	23
Haircut	24
Uncle Henry	26
Mother Justice	28
The County Fair	30
Old Friends	32
Grandfather's Shotgun	33
Croup	35
Witch	36
My Dreams Are Strong	38
Mulberries	39
Leppy	40
Paper Route	42
Foot Race	44
Garden	46

II. The Teenager

First Cigarette	51
West Park	52
The Black Strap	54
Horse Chestnuts	56
Her Sister Loretta	58

Alice   60
Fourth of July   62
Amber Indian   64
Summer Heat   66
Saturday Morning   68
Trapped in the Corner   70
Blue Heron Lake   72
Tracks   75
Linda   76

III. The Old Man

I Remember Arizona   79
Walking to School   80
Geese   81
Father's Story   82
Uncle Ernest   83
Charles and Lydia   84
Fox Robe   85
Old Photos   86
Cousin Barbara   88
In Prayers   89
Cemetery in Towamencin   90
Lydia's Sampler   91
Midwinter   92
In the Dream I See Franklin Street, 93

I.
The Kid

Franklin Street, 1957

The rag man, in his broken shoes
pushes his cart along the brick street,
calls out with chafed voice,
"Papers, magazines, rags."

All afternoon the air is still and pale,
the yellow leaves pasted to the wet street.

Near dusk, Schmoyer's farm truck
clanks onto Franklin Street,
loaded with cabbages, and carrots,
potatoes with the mud still on.

The old women gather, make piles
on the wooden truck bed.
He places the vegetables into brown bags
with his broad hands,
the tips of his thumbs split at the nails.

My mother just called him Schmoyer.
I never knew his first name.

Leonard the egg man, with his poor toupee
parks his black wagon half on the sidewalk.

Sadie Bauer loads her splint basket with brown eggs
and a loaf of earthy brown bread.

Schmoyer hands me a big red apple.

Heavy rain from the west
will soon gush in the gutters,
wash black ants from the bowed heads
of the white peonies.

At Age 5

Judy showed me her underpants.

Naughty, naughty we hid in the bushes
behind her house
under the grape arbor
with the dog watching and Grammy Cope

just inside washing dishes—
Grammy Cope, the Mennonite housekeeper
in her ankle-length black dress
and blue apron,

her white cap covering her white hair,
her clumsy black shoes, then clopping across the porch.
She peeked over the railing and growled,
Wicked, wicked, wicked! You go in the house, and you go home!

I wet my pants
and ran home crying
through the back yard
and into my room.

As I undressed, my shoe laces tangled.
With the knots too tight to undo,
I yanked them off
and tossed them

into the corner
with the Dick and Jane books,
crawled under the covers,

pinched my eyes closed,
and disappeared.

Glass Button

Grandmother's gray wool winter coat was topped
with a glorious green glass button.
It was oblong and transparent, large enough to fill a child's hand.

To a six-year-old it was treasure, and in my naivety
I asked if I could have it when she died.
I don't recall her response but felt certain
I would be written into her will. The deal was sealed.

It was not.

When she died years later her effects were distributed
to relatives and the second-hand store.
Later, when it was too late, I recalled the glass button.

Over time I came to realize
I did not need the object but could learn
to carry the memory of her
like the melancholy strains
of Barber's *Adagio*.

Funeral

Grandpa Z turned in
his conductor hat
at the trolley car company in 1935.

He bought a restaurant on Eighth Street
and began simmering oyster stew,
baking beans, and serving pie.

The month before, he knew nothing
about running a business,
little about cooking a meal,
but he learned.

Pie brings them back,
but beans is where the money is.

I remember him after church, a stocky man
with a white bristle mustache, self-assured
in his Sunday blue trousers and vest
over a starched white shirt,

tending a joint of beef,
sampling a sliver from one end
while it crisped in the oven.

In the afternoon we played Old Maid.
He always knew when I held the Maid card.
He grinned and whispered,
Electric Lights.

He died when I was seven.
His was the first funeral I attended,
him pale and quiet
in the full blue suit.

I touched his hand, no longer natural.

My brother whispered,
don't do that.

Sleep Ritual

I hold the rabbit close, whisper,
ask for safe passage
to the place of shadow things.

If I stay in a certain face-down position,
with legs extended, feet pointed,
arms along my sides, fingers curled,

and if I believe, without wavering,
then I can rise and glide
over Mrs. Moyer's hedge,

soar above the trees,
the curling creek,
the tiny birds that watch below

and ease down
my bare belly
onto the green summer grass.

The Cellar

Grandma sent me down the creaky wooden steps
to fetch jars of dilly beans and pickled beets

which aroused my anxiety because
there was a monkey paw in the back corner.
Not so menacing by daylight
but after dark, that's when the thing came alive.

It was just a fuzzy hunk of brown insulation
on a water pipe, half hidden by a tapestry of cobwebs,
but it moved a little when dim light
from the bare bulb lit its fur.

Beneath it, mortar fell from the stone walls.
Its moisture attracting centipedes
and the occasional cricket which chirped
the same sound a monkey paw would make.

Hip boots hung from a hook behind the Masonite cabinet
stocked with canned goods, mouse traps, and flypaper.
They looked like baggy pants—
a dark man who watched over the crock
of fermenting sauerkraut.

The hole in the wall near the ceiling
was the place where the snake could crawl in.

Haircut

The tall brick house belonging to my grandmother,
sat beneath silver maples and linden trees.
It was where I lived out my childhood,

and where, in the first-floor bathroom, I suffered haircuts
at the hands of my impatient father.

Quit rutching!

At least once he nipped me with the gun-metal scissors.
The electric clipper, a shade of dark maroon
buzzed next to my ear, felt warm on my neck.

Though he covered me with a striped sheet,
the tiny clipped hairs found their way under
and picked at my neck and back.

Keep still!

Always the sides were shorn too short,
my exposed scalp looking like the belly of our old dog.
The top was combed back with Vitalis Hair Tonic
so I looked like the kid on the cover of *Boy's Life* magazine.

To keep from flinching
I imagined being chased by a gang of hoods with pistols.

I pictured hiding among trash barrels in the alley
behind the row houses in our neighborhood.
If I moved, I was a goner.

Dad, being a perfectionist, snipped and snipped
until there was almost nothing left.
When he was finally finished, he had me stand
before the mirror so that we could admire his work.

Then he gave me a dime for an ice cream cone
at Acker's corner grocery.

Uncle Henry

He scared us when he gave us a ride
in the bucket of his front-end loader,
lifted us up to the ceiling of the barn, gave us a shake
while his spaniel Duke watched from below.

We had the run of his tree nursery and the fields beyond,
wild with rabbits and Chinese pheasants.

He had a Nazi dagger with a swastika on the handle
and a silver bullet wired to a tag that read,
"The Bullet That Killed Hitler."

At Christmas, in his rathskeller with the stone fireplace
and straps of sleigh bells, he laid out an ice cream bar,
gallon buckets and toppings—strawberry, chocolate,
butterscotch, nuts and whipped cream.
His rule was, *Eat all you want.*

He had a Christmas tree stand on Hamilton Street
with fir trees and pines and holly wreaths with red berries.

His Aunt Sarah came from Lancaster to manage the stand
in her fur-topped galoshes and wire-rimmed glasses,
her red hair up in a bun fixed with a blue glass hat pin.

When I visited the stand, she gave me a molasses cookie.
He pulled me aside and handed me a two-dollar bill saying,
Funny money.

When I was in 3rd grade, the sudden news came that he had died.
I didn't know he was sick.
Cancer.
He was 51.

By the time of his funeral, I was cried out.
Across the room from the casket I sat in silence,
my shoes, polished that morning by my dad,
tucked beneath the seat, while my cheek
was cleaned by Mother's dampened handkerchief.
The place smelled of mums, smelled like every funeral.
Slow, dim organ music played in the walls,
the people milled about, shook hands, nodded,
whispered something.

After the last prayer, family and friends gathered
at Grandmother's house. In her parlor, tables were set
tea and punch, finger sandwiches.

Stories were told. There was a smattering of laughter.
I sat on the carpet under the piano and rubbed Duke's ears.
They should have had an ice cream bar.

Mother Justice

When Teddy's kickoff sailed over the fence
into Alma Kutcher's yard, she flew from the back door
and seized the ball, tucked it under her arm,
her mouth curling in contempt.

She carried the ball into the house and glowered
through the window as she continued to wash her dishes.

Dejected, we returned home, sulking about in the back yard.
Mother asked, *Why so glum?*

When we told her, off she went,
tossed open Mrs. Kutcher's gate,
rapped her knuckles on the back door,
stood with hands on hips until Mrs. Kutcher appeared,
football in one hand, dish towel in the other,

What the hell do you want?
Mom said, *I'll take the ball for starters,
and a kinder face would be nice.*

In an instant the dish towel snapped into Mother's face,
and just as quick the towel was snatched
and the ball knocked to the ground.

Mother picked it up and was through the gate
toting dish towel and ball while we watched from the alley.

We followed her home in triumph,
a silent parade.

The County Fair

Each autumn we hopped the fence at the county fair
eager for the freak shows and girlie shows, the food concessions,
and the Mighty Atom.

The Atom was strongman Joseph Greenstein.
His voice coursed through an antique microphone
strapped to his gray beard, the texture of Shredded Wheat.

Displayed were newspaper clippings—
proof that he pulled a truck uphill with his long hair,
broke chains locked around his chest.

From the tailgate of his 1940s Dodge flatbed,
he extolled the benefits of the healthy life
maintained with "Redemption Tonic"
that he could provide for a dollar.

He held a few 10" spikes in one hand
passed some for the gathered crowd to test.

Sweat dripped from his face onto his crinkled hairy chest
as he began to bend a spike wrapped in a stained handkerchief.
In time it took on a curve and then was u-shaped.

Never mind the girlie shows, skinny teens
dancing on the stage in gaudy gauze costumes,
never mind the Fat Man, or Shultzy the Pin Head.

We went for The Mighty Atom!

Not because he was strong
but because he was old like a wind-bent tree,
his voice rattled with authenticity,
his accent said he was from afar.

Years later I came to learn
that he was Polish and a Jew,
meaningful in those years just after the war,
a survivor of persistent persecution,

as were his ancestors
in Russia, in Poland, Croatia—
the old lands.

And finally, I discovered, in my own ancestry,
names I did not hear from my parents,
but names of family from the 1600s,
not German names,

for there was no Germany then, but Silesia,
the land that would later become
Germany and Poland, the code in my own genes,
the life force of Ashkenazi Jews.

Old Friends

In her tired house dress,
Miss Gertie settles into a wicker rocker
beside grandmother,
among snake plants
in red clay pots.

Homely as an old mule,
I thought she was a man,
her white chopped hair,
gravel voice,
her bristled chin.

She seems small inside her clothes
since her fall,
listing, uncertain,
her breath like curdled milk.

And then no breath.

Grandmother gazes from the window,
clasps the green glass button
of her heavy coat.

The black fingers of the linden tree
scratch against the rain spout
as the wind rises.

Grandfather's Shotgun

As a boy, A.C. sailed, with parents and five siblings
from Wiesbaden in 1858.
He died before I was born.

He drove a 1928 Chevrolet but stabled his chestnut bay
in the mud-floor garage behind the house
where he smoked his fat cigars.

His shotgun was a Parker Brothers
Damascus steel double barrel,
hand-carved walnut stock.

He spoke softly, I was told,
baritone tinged with German,
gray eyes beneath his stern hawk brow.

On a Saturday morning, age eight,
I spied the shotgun
beneath the green iron daybed in the forbidden attic.

I slipped it from its leather case
and hefted its weight to my shoulder,
felt for the trigger.

Taking aim,
from the tall, rattly window,
that faced the back alley,

I took out Old Man Heil.
Winged him, actually.
He didn't notice.

Croup

If I wake hoarse and barking,
Grandma catches me by the elbow
and collects her kit from the whatnot shelf.
The brown tin cup is placed
on the cast iron grill
over the blue gas flame.
A finger of translucent ointment
fished from the blue jar
is wiped into the cup to melt.
She rolls a newspaper cone
to concentrate the assault
of vapors rising in the air,
wavery like a washboard.
Ice splinters shock my nasal passages,
eyes pinch and lungs suddenly expand.
There is no escape.
A gob of Vicks is smeared into
my honey hollow, a brindle rag
is wrapped around my throat.
Oatmeal with raisins and brown sugar
is ladled into an earthenware bowl
with a yellow rooster painted on the side.
There will be no school for me today after all.

Witch

Through my mother, Mrs. Haberstroh
hired me to take out her garbage, little as it was.
I was 8, scared of witches and for sure, she was a witch.

I had seen her at her parlor window,
her white hair, coiled on top of her head
pinned with amber barrettes.

Tuesday was the day she would put
the brown paper bag on the wicker bench
on her front porch, a dime beside the bag.

At 7 a.m. I walked two blocks to her house,
a tall Victorian place with stained glass windows
and overgrown shrubs that guarded her gate.

I watched from across 15th Street,
hidden behind her neighbor's black Buick,
to be sure she was not outside waiting.

But as I approached, the tall door opened
and she stepped out—
her pale, powdered face,

pernicious wet eyes and red lipstick,
a brocade shawl across her shoulders,
a long black velvet skirt.

She stood between me and the bench,
just as I had imagined.
I ran.

At home my mother insisted that I make good
on my agreement, but she never acknowledged
the fact that Mrs. Haberstroh was indeed a witch.

In the weeks that followed, I did carry her garbage
to the curb and pocketed the dime.
But I never saw her again.

She died a short while later.
My parents attended her funeral,
but I didn't.

My Dreams Are Strong

They grab me in the dark
and carry me to vague childhood spaces,

that acidic thin man towers, fedora, no eyes,
I'm pressed into the corner of the dim room

with the lamb-colored wall paper,
suffocating in sick morning light,

a bilious smell,
a scratching at the shutters.

The crier crow on the railroad fence
calls forth the persistent day.

Mulberries

I remember orchids through the window
of a solarium's silver glass,
on Ruben Patterson's property—his estate,

with its mammoth mansion,
with its broad veranda and 4-car garage,
his cream and gold Stutz Bearcat.

The meticulous perennial beds in back were flush
with stands of columbine, foxglove, bearded iris,
rooted beneath the mulberry tree I climbed
to pick sweet, dark berries, purple stains
across the chest of my white t-shirt,
ever the risk that he would arrive home

while I was high in the tree and catch me.
As much as the mulberries, the adrenaline rush
was a draw, spawning images in my mind—

the police cruiser, lights flashing,
the police station,
the Juvie Cop, his pack of Lucky Strikes on the desk,

his Zippo and a heavy glass ashtray,
sweated, detained until my parents could bail me
back to freedom, acting remorseful and contrite.

Leppy

Everyone called him Leppy.
He had a skin disease like leprosy
and a high husk in his voice.

His rotund belly too large to fit most cars,
he drove a late model Oldsmobile,
a boat of a car with style.

He ate half a smoked ham joint at a sitting.
His brother Eddy ate the other half
when they celebrated Easter.
Church was not involved.

He played the ponies, but back from the track
too late on a Sunday night, he didn't make it
to the nursery on Monday.

Dad brought Leppy to our place once
to help plant shrubs in the side yard.
You'd have to say he was jolly.

By day's end, he was soaked with sweat.
Since he wouldn't fit in the cab, they took him home
in the bed of a '59 Chevy pickup.

Before he left,
he handed me a shiny dime,
said, *Buy a comic or something,
don't gamble it away.*

Paper Route

Mr. Fenstamaker wanted his paper wedged
between the pickets of his wrought iron fence,
by 7 a.m. sharp. That did not always happen.

Meryl Hendricks wanted hers inside the screen door.
Her dog, Lefty barked like crazy when the door slammed,
So don't slam the damn door!

Lewis Larisch was my boss.
I thought of him as Lewie The Larisch
as if a larisch was some sort of animal,
sort of a plump rat in a molting fur coat.

It was also my job to collect and record payments
from my customers which I did on Saturdays
riding my bike through the row house neighborhoods.

Some customers pretended not to be home,
In apartment hallways with peeling wall paper
and the stench of boiled cabbage, some shouted,
Come back tomorrow.

The saving grace was collecting from Reppert's Bar.
Bud Reppert always sat me on a stool and brought a cold root beer
in a pilsner glass. He paid in cash and included a dollar tip.

In winter the sky was dark when my alarm sounded.
The air, cold and quiet.
The milk truck squished through the slushy streets.

Grimm's Bakery delivered donuts to the dairy's metal milk box.
I stole a donut as Mrs. Newton watched from the window
in her bedraggled terry cloth robe. An unfiltered Chesterfield
hung from her pallid lips.

Mr. Larisch came to my house the next Saturday
to retrieve my collection book, canvas bag and hole punch.
I never knew what the hole punch was for.

He said he was sorry, said he too had a hard time
getting up in the dark, said he too stole donuts
when he was a paperboy, said
the trick is, don't get caught.

Foot Race

Most Saturdays Albert showed up in the alley
behind Freddy Schmerker's house—
a middle-aged man dressed in a dark blue suit
and polished black captoes, jacket over his arm
like a waiter in an Old World restaurant,
graying hair slicked back, pocket full of dimes.

The dimes were for bets on foot races against any of us
in our high tops, dungarees turned up, white t-shirts.
He never won. He always paid.

Albert lived with a brother in their deceased parent's brick
row house on Franklin Street. He was soft-spoken and nervous.
We knew nothing more about him. After the races he sat
on the curb with us. No one spoke.

Albert was skinny and hunched, had big hands
that he used to slice the air when he ran.
He hung his jacket over the fuchsia Rose of Sharon
in Mrs. Bechdol's yard.
When he rolled up his pants cuffs we noticed
his white bony ankles. He wore no socks.

Eddy said, *He must be batty. Who comes in a suit*
to race kids and bet on it to boot,
lose every race, and come back again?

Some of us tried to race twice but no dice.

Summer wore into fall, and after the County Fair
school began again, and we forgot about racing Albert.

On a day in October the news came.
Dressed in a business suit and polished dress shoes,
Albert Cassone died after a fall from the 8th Street bridge.
He was predeceased by his beloved younger sister, Camilla,
and is survived by older brother, Martin.

We never spoke of him after that
but I thought of him when I bought my first suit.

Garden

Fred Wormly looked like Mississippi John Hurt,
had the same dark mahogany voice.

He lived by the community gardens.
His plot was verdant and weed-free,
with 20 kinds of vegetables,
nasturtiums and strawberries.

On his splint basket for surplus,
a hand-painted notice.
Take a few of what you need
and some you jiss want.

Missing a couple of front teeth
his smile flashed with one gold incisor.

He wore baggy khakis with a blue work shirt,
a crumpled dust-colored fedora, and creased,
heavy work shoes well-rubbed with neatsfoot oil.

In the middle of Saturday cartoons
Mom sent me to gather tomatoes and spinach,

but as I was heading home,
Fred called to me on the dirt path,
asked me to join him for a plate.
Boiled potatoes and green beans.

Ruth is gone, just me and Sadie now.

After greeting me with her long tail
Sadie curled up under the table.
She was missing a couple of front teeth too.

He told me stories including how she came to him
sent by the Holy Spirit. And Ruth.

He sent me home with one red tomato and one yellow,
and asked if my folks would let me have a dog.
We're both old, he said, *don't know which of us will go first.*

II.
The Teenager

First Cigarette

Bare legs hanging over
the edge of the garage roof,
skinny Measle White takes a drag
on the Pall Mall,
coughs like a clogged lawnmower.

Teddy Fritz strikes a Bogart pose,
heavy eyelids,
cig between thumb and forefinger.

Chippy lets a smoke feather
trail from her delicious lips,

lips on the cover of *Detective Magazine,*
the guy looming,
the woman bent back.

We walk Chippy under the linden trees,
sit on her porch,
no one ready to go home

to Dad parking the Plymouth,
the squatty white dog shivering with joy,
ham and boiled cabbage,
Grandma calling in the dark
for a little sip of water.

West Park

The old lady had a brown paper bag
full of peanuts in the shell, feeding gray and blue pigeons
gathered by her feet like a flock of parishioners,
their guttural cooing, warbling prayers of gratitude.

The chunky ill-mannered squirrels snatched
all their paws could hold and hauled
up the trunk of the maple overhanging the fountain.

The peanut lady wore a lavender dress imprinted
with small flowers, and a wide-brimmed straw hat
with a dark feather in the band.

Nearby was a band shell where the town band played
for the gathered elderly on certain Sundays after church,
pieces composed for trombone, tuba, and kettle drum.

Under duress I sometimes accompanied my grandmother
to these events to protect her from stumbling
on the uneven sidewalk, lifted and tilted by the tree roots beneath.

The peanut lady was napping now, her chin on her chest,
a squirrel beside her on the bench, the bag between his teeth
as he dragged it to the ground, spilling the contents,
which created a free-for-all.

Dark purple clouds gathered in the western sky,
a few large drops pelted leaves,
dimpled the fountain pool,
woke the peanut lady.

She wrapped her shoulders with the oatmeal cardigan
from her canvas bag, and hastened from the park.

I wondered if she lived alone, wondered if she lived nearby,
wondered if I would someday sit on a park bench
with a bag of peanuts and a straw hat, old and quiet.

The Black Strap

We snitched coins from the Japanese lacquer tray
on Father's dresser,
cigarettes from Mother's pocketbook.

Sometimes we drove her to the edge.
"Don't make me get the black strap."

Manners were taught by father.

Napkin folded on the lap.
No elbows on the dinner table.
No singing.
Robert hummed.
No humming.

Shave a pat of butter,
place it on the edge of your bread plate.
Slice two or three bites from your
piece of the roast, not more.

Don't talk with your mouth full.
Do not burp. Or worse.
Don't interrupt.
Don't hold your fork like a screwdriver.
Ask to be excused from the table.
Thank your mother.

The strap was taken from its hook just once.

Mother chased Robert through the kitchen,
down the hall,
up the front stairs,
down the back stairs,
out the back door,
into the side yard
where he mounted his Schwinn
and rode off.

She collapsed on the porch glider crying.

I sat beside her and took the strap from her clenched fingers.
I hung it back in the pantry closet, beside her apron
with the Dutch Girl stitched on the front.

Horse Chestnuts

The best place to collect horse chestnuts
was behind the Lutheran church.

The prickly pods looked like sea urchins.
Pried open they revealed mahogany brown treasures
that gave off the aroma of cashews and shoe polish.

Inside the church Reverend Pflum offered monotonous sermons
about the Lord and the disciples and the donkeys.

One Sunday, Jonesy whispered to me: *Pflum's left ear
is bigger than the right, the earlobe hangs over his collar.*

I was infected by slow laughter,
that grew and burbled through my nose.
From the last row we were able to escape with little notice.

We spent our offering money on Mars Bars and Black Jack Gum
in Gerard S. Mest's drugstore, then gathered a few chestnuts.

On the way home Jonesy swiped a pack of cigs
from an open car, reached a freckled hand into his shirt pocket
and pulled out a lighter, lit one
and blew a stream of blue smoke into the air.

It did not end with cigarettes.

Her Sister Loretta

I rode along with my grandmother
to retrieve her sister
dying of cancer in Coatesville.

Sister Loretta, now but a bag of twigs,
curled silently on the wide back seat
of Aunt Maggie's powder-blue Lincoln.

Bored with the billboards,
I asked if the Lincoln could do 90.
In red high heels she showed me
that it sure could.
I have no recollection of anything else
from that day.

Loretta was settled into the room at the top
of the wooden stairs—the dark room
that overlooked row houses where the heat
of August shimmered from the gray slate roofs.

While the aging neighbors waved paper fans
from some recent funeral at the Lutheran church,
Sister Loretta's belly tightened and swelled
under her strangled green nightgown.
Her voice trailed off, watery and slow,
her vowels tender as egg custard.

She died for two weeks in that room
that smelled like wet wallpaper
and White Cloverine Salve.

After she passed I brushed her hand.
It felt like the bark
of a beech tree in winter.

Alice

The widow Abigail Bitting lived for 66 years
in her brown brick house.
She wore her deceased husband's brogans
and baggy pants scented with bacon grease.

Her side yard was awash with irises and lilies
beneath the honeysuckle where hummingbirds
hovered among blossoms and vines.

Her white hair beneath a blue bonnet,
she sang soft psalms in German
while she unearthed weeds
and tossed them on the compost pile.

Her tow-headed granddaughter Alice
spent a week with her each summer,
and each summer I was drawn across the alley
to the privet hedge for long talks with Alice
about everything, about nothing.

She lived in Milwaukee, a distant planet.
She played violin and loved math.
We played what is the square root of . . .

Alice wore dresses
and smelled like sliced apples.

I was different around her,
a boy she lured into being.

In August her father came for her
in his station wagon,
a brown and white dog
hanging out the window.

Though I knew Alice was gone,
I looked for her each time I passed

while the widow Bitting
knelt among the lilies and irises,
softly singing to herself.

Fourth of July

Fat Ralph's green Packard sat in the alley like a ship in dry dock
because there was no room in the garage
where he stored the beach umbrella,
bikes, scooters, and the chain-driven ice cream maker
which now churned the cream and sugar
in its rotating steel barrel
inside a core of ice and rock salt.

The stars and stripes hung from porch posts.
We strapped on black, silver-studded holsters,
slipped long-barreled cap guns into the leather breach.

The street buzzed with energy more palpable than patriotism.
Kids wheeled out their carbide cannons over-filled
with the granular powder that exploded when sparked
and put up a puff of acrid, sulphur-smelling smoke.

Stevie Snyder had firecrackers brought from Canada.
Jack lit one on his sneaker to see what it would do,
then hopped all around yowling.

The Mummers Parade was broadcast from Philadelphia,
the Mummers marching in hand-made costumes fashioned in silk,
feathers and shiny swathes of glitter,
playing banjos and bass drums and glockenspiels.

When aromas rose across the neighborhood
from charcoal grills where hot dogs and burgers roasted,
paper plates were piled with potato salad, pickles and chips,
and later star-spangled cakes beside bowls
of Ralph's yellowish vanilla ice cream.

At dusk the migration to the football stadium began.
The bleachers filled, while others set up lawn chairs on the hills.
When floodlights went dark, the sky lit up with explosions
and sparkles in the shapes of stars and chrysanthemums,
the loud reports coming a second or two after the flash.

The day morphed into a dream,
protocols and curfews suspended.
The crowd moseyed home along dim streets,
voices became a furry mumbling in the distance.

Amber Indian

When the weather warmed
and the sky held big white clouds,
we rode bikes to the estate of Reuben Butz.

If his Mercedes
was not in the garage,
we went exploring.

There was a wide veranda in front
where tall windows
allowed a view into the living room.

There were Persian rugs and antique furniture,
but of most interest was the amber figure
on the cherry drop-leaf table—

a translucent Indian
with a feathered headdress,
glowing with sunlight.

Eugene disappeared, but soon
we saw him through the window
moving slowly through the living room.

He tiptoed across the polished wood floor
and took the figure from the table.
pushed it into his jeans pocket.

Outside we examined it for a long time,
the way light brought it alive,
then begged him to put it back,

but when we heard the Mercedes coming
we mounted our bikes and raced
across the grass to the creek and into the trees.

Eugene agreed to return the figure
the next time we went exploring
on the old man's property.

The following Saturday
I spied the Indian in the window
of Robert Sadler's pawn shop.

Summer Heat

The sky is swelled with heat.
There is no breeze.
Even the sparrows are in siesta.

I bounce a tennis ball against the brick wall
of the house where I live
with my grandmother and her plants.

I smash a black ant
under the heel of my sneaker,
then another and another.

In the backyard
a patrol of yellow jackets emerges
from the collapsed brick fire pit.

With a stave from a broken peach basket
I swat them dead, one after another.
They find me and sting my arms and neck.
They inject fire.

I hike along Mill Creek with Danny and Jack.
We come upon spring snakes
on the rock shelf that overhangs the creek.
Danny's walking stick sends one over the edge.

Jack, pulls a can of lighter fluid
from the pocket of his denim jacket,
squirts a stream onto the remaining snake,
lights a stick match and tosses it onto the wet coil.

As flames burst, it writhes and twists and bubbles.
After that, I stop killing things.

Saturday Morning

Saturday morning Teddy Redmane
skids into my side yard
on his Schwinn Cruiser.
In his knapsack, American cheese on white
with yellow mustard
and Tasty Kake peach pies.

I tie off the cuff of my dungarees
so it won't catch in the chain
and swing my leg over
like my bike is a pony.

We ride to Helfrich Springs today
to look for snakes and frogs
and trout in the waving current of Cedar Creek.

We pass row houses on Franklin Street,
take the dirt road under the big maples,
coast in the quiet shade,
then without a word, come to a halt.

Above, a red tail studies the clearing,
head turns slowly.
He releases and glides into the thicket below.

The road drops quickly now,
and we keep brakes pinched.
At the bottom, with bikes laid into underbrush
we climb out onto the flat rock
that overhangs the creek.

And there they are. Half a dozen speckled brook trout
holding on the slow edge of the flow.
They suck mayflies from the surface.
The creek carries the occasional moth,
rice paper wings stuck to the water,
thread-thin legs point to heaven.

We watch clouds shift shape,
strip and slip into the rushing stream.
And then the snake.

A fat brown water snake, long as a ball bat,
head held aloft, swims like a side winder.
We toss a few pebbles to speed it along.

Dried by clean air and sunshine, we pull on shorts and sneaks,
hike a worn path among mosses and acorn crowns.
This bit of forest is familiar
with natural benches and hidden huts,
sanctuaries of spiders with webs strong as mending thread,
colonies of red ants.

A kingfisher lights on a maple branch, silver minnow in her beak.
In late afternoon we resurrect bikes, push them uphill
to level ground and ride home,
tired and satisfied
as we will ever be.

Trapped in the Corner

He chanted, "Owzo, hurtzo, trapped in the corner like a ratso."
And he was, in the stairwell between classes,
Bennie Bankovic and Wilbur Spang
giving him knuckle punches
on his arms and shoulders.

With his palsied hand folded into his chest
like an injured bird,
the polio leg he dragged
along the polished terrazzo floors,

his full lips and brown eyes,
his curly black hair covering his temples,
Mark Caspar was beautiful
and grotesque—
and a wizard with numbers.

The two boys referred to him as Spaz 2.
Spaz 1 was Emily Suzanne,
also known as Twist and Shout,
her upper body and legs
at odds, twisting in opposite directions
when she walked.

Mark sat near Emily in algebra class.
He watched her twirling the ends of her brown hair.

He thought she had pretty lips.

He imagined walking her home after school,
along Franklin Street under the linden trees,
how their hands would brush,
how he would say smart things and make her smile,
take her to Nelson's Ice Cream for a sundae.

Emily wore a brace on her leg and a corrective shoe,
something in common, a way to start,
not with words, he thought, but a private glance.

On Friday Mark walked to the circle in Willow Park,
sat on one of the green iron benches
near the fountain to watch the pigeons, the odd way
they bobbed their heads when they walked
and gargled soft sounds.

Blue Heron Lake

I woke at dawn.
Still beneath the musty quilt
I cranked the tall window open,
smelled the moist air coming off the lake.

I stretched and stepped from the bed,
pulled on jeans and sneakers,
the green flannel shirt over my white t-shirt
and crept down the stairs to avoid waking the adults.

I grabbed a muffin and an apple
and hurried to the lakeside
where the wooden rowboat was moored,
rods and tackle set in the night before.

It was the first year I was allowed to take the boat out
by myself. I stepped one foot in and pushed off from the shore.

A wispy mist rose from the black lake,
the boat made a cushing sound
as it glided through the still water.

A heron fished in the shallows,
its stiff legs reflected in the surface.

I watched silver-blue minnows drift
amid the swaying grasses,
heard the familiar clank of the oarlocks
as I dipped the sculpted oars into the dark water.

I rowed to the small island at the far end,
rested the prow against a broad, gray rock
just above the surface.

Chain pickerel cruised in the lily pad forest.
Sunfish, with blue and orange iridescent scales
reflected the early sun
as they turned above their nests.
On the first cast, my lure was torn from the line
by something that swirled the water
and disappeared below.

The fourth cast fooled a good-sized bass,
my racing line cut the surface,
the tug of the fish excited me.

I landed the thick black fish, admired its muscle and shine
as it lay on the floor of the boat,
its mouth pulling for air.

I unhooked and released the bass
into the tannin-stained water
and rested my rod on the wooden seat.

In the silence, I noticed a pair of golden frog eyes
just above the water,
a green nose, shiny and wet.

Dragonflies hovered and dipped
among the yellow lily blossoms,
curled their segmented tails.

Hidden birds called from the leafy trees,
as the morning warmed,
and thick white clouds collected above.

I felt something new come upon me and opened to it.
No longer separate from the world around me
the world was within, and I was the world.

I felt a stirring in my loins,
smiled into the sky and tingled.

Tracks

In August heat,
the sibilation of cicadas
intensifies, stops.

Silence.

In black high tops
we hike the trestle above the creek,
center pennies on the steel rail,
sit in shade with whittled walking sticks.

The shrill whistle,
the steel wheels,
the clatter and shake.

Pennies now warm in the cinders,
stretched wafers,
Lincoln with a longer beard.

We try curse words,
repeat stories told by an uncle
around the campfire—

the rabid dog,
the half-deer woman,
the escapee with the hook.

In the dusk we trek home,
to the pot roast, the unmown lawn,
"Paladin."

Linda

We stood gazing into the pond when I noticed
she was holding a bouquet of tiny lavender flowers.

I had been watching for fish just beneath the surface,
Japanese koi glinting in the sunlight.

Where did you find the flowers?
You're standing in them.

When she was 13, I left home,
missing out on her teen years.

She wed in a meadow in Maine
while I was in Southeast Asia.

I pictured her in a long calico dress,
beside Billy, smiling at the whole sky,

holding a bouquet of tiny wild flowers.

III.
The Old Man

I Remember Arizona

The old western movies felt warmed through with sunshine
and puffing white clouds overhead as the cowboys
rode their mustangs through canyons of red rock,
saguaro cactus taking a stand with arms akimbo
on the yellow sand, hot on the trail of outlaws and Indians
in a quest to secure the lands called Arizona, Montana, Wyoming.

I wanted to ride with them, six-gun in my leather holster,
bullwhip at the ready, curry comb and rations in my saddle bag,
bedroll cinched across my horse's rump, canteen, lariat, rifle.
My posse would include Hank and Clint, Buck and Billie.

At night we'd have dried beef and bannock from the chuck wagon,
snorts of whiskey, and Slim singing songs around the campfire,
harmonica melancholy across the dark prairie, coyotes howling
in the distance, stories of close calls with the biggest rattlers,
and a horse hobbled by a gopher hole, then needing to be shot.

Flying arrows, wagons set on fire,
swinging saloon doors, poker chips on a felt-topped table,
the Mexican sidekick dying by the waterhole
with the skull sign obscured by sagebrush.

Finally, the train, curdled smoke pouring from its stack,
chugging through the barren landscape carrying the mail
and wanted posters to Kansas City just as the Dalton Gang
rides off to their hideout in the foothills
near the abandoned ranch and the silver mine.

I live in Arizona now, but it's not the same
as I remember in "3:10 To Yuma."

Walking to School

This early autumn morning
there is a warm, yellow-gray pane
at the horizon
behind the towering chestnut
that guards the row houses on Franklin Street.

I am reminded of the year
my Uncle Ernest died.

Melancholy is stitched into the collective conscious,
a contented resignation
more felt than realized,
like the vacancy left
when the hummingbirds have flown.

Fallen leaves on the black pavement,
the smell of latent rain,
my pocket full of chestnuts
that will be arranged
on the tin cover of the iron radiator
that ticks in the night.
Early on we learn to escape
the palpability of grief.

Geese

Early mornings in autumn
father would burst into our sleep,
throw open the window
shouting, "Geese, boys, geese!"

We could hear them in the distance,
their reedy voices
like swelling war hoops
come into focus.

His head outside the window,
he studied the grey sky.
Bent at the waist
in boxers and strap t-shirt,
he would estimate their number.
Announce it.

And then they were right overhead,
deep clarinet, saxophone, flying low enough
to hear their soft gray wings wave against the air.

At that moment nothing in the world mattered to him
until they vanished into the atmosphere,
their last notes whittled thin and faint.

He is gone now too,
but every autumn I picture the door flung open,
and I hear those words.

Father's Story

He described memories of his father with his smoke-yellow teeth,
smooth palms, white mustache thick over his lip—
a man who ran a restaurant, served
the lady of the night
cloaked in fox fur

chamomile tea in the dark corner, steel
and iron sounds from across the river,
alleyways and oak oyster barrels,

a small pistol beneath the cash register,
the basement floor
of packed earth and coal dust,

feathers of a quail,
pelt of a rabbit,
beak of a goose

nailed to the rafters—
charms against
wicked spirits.

Uncle Ernest

was a thin man, bent crane-like.
His Adam's apple
bobbed with his keening harangue.
Also when he laughed.
A bank clerk, he was invested,
AT&T, U.S. Steel.
He died alone in the shower,
discovered by the mail carrier two days later,
the water running cold by now.
He willed the bulk of his estate
to a TV evangelist,
all but the $1000 to my father
and the $1000 to an Indian school in South Dakota,
a place he had visited during the one vacation
of his 40-year banking career.

A holocaust denier,
we argued until he turned crimson,
and slammed out the door.
Decades later,
Indian boarding schools made the news,
their process, their purpose.

Charles and Lydia

The sepia photo of my great grandparents,
is their only record beyond their headstones.

I imagine the soft flesh of her wrists,
her ginger hair curls like a French horn,
Charles as white as a cod without his shirt.

As she lays her smock across the maple rocker,
the casual yellow dog watches discreetly,
his chin on the braided rug.

They slip beneath the muslin sheet,
exhale and smile.

In this bed she conceived their ninth child,
the same day she became a grandmother.

Fox Robe

Grandma called it the fox robe.

I found it in the steamer trunk
in her attic
wrapped in brown butcher paper.

It was more of a blanket. Eight fox pelts
with glass eyes, a hint of fine yellow teeth.

Unrolled, it released the aroma of moth balls
intended to prevent moths from eating the foxes.

The trunk brought my grandfather's belongings
from Germany in 1878.

The robe covered Grandmother's lap
when he courted her in his black buggy.

How fine they looked, her in a round fur hat,
him in his tall, tan Stetson and clenched cigar.

At age 19, she agreed to marry him.
He was 34.

He died before I was born,
leaving her the house where I grew up.

When it was time,
I inherited the trunk.
By then the moths had won.

Old Photos

In a grease-stained biscuit box in the attic
I find packets of old photos,
some with names penciled on the back.

My grandfather wears a brown fedora,
hoists a string of pickerel,
their soft slippery tails
wet against his boot.

In another he wears a dark necktie,
shirt buttoned to the throat,
as he cradles his shotgun.

Two limp Chinese pheasants
hang from his wide belt,
a black cigar clamped in his teeth.

In this picture, Grandmother stares
from a filigreed silver frame,
her ivory-yellow hair coiled,
a soft mole on her powdered cheek,

this grandmother I lived with,
this grandmother I took for granted like furniture,
now pale and shrunken,
not much bigger than a child.

Soon relatives and friends
in Sunday clothes,
silent in the hallway,

dark carpets and heavy drapes,
the piquant smell of mums,
hushed voices, everything in slow motion.

Cousin Barbara

From the orange crate in the attic
I have brought sepia photos she has never seen.
Barbara, my older cousin I fell in love with
at age ten, her golden hair and red lipstick.

Pictures of her own father in the early years
when he rented tents
to the carnies at the great fair,
the girlie shows, the freak shows.

Among the wills and patents, photos
of our shared grandmother in a red cloche hat
perched on the leather seat of Grandpa's buggy,
the dusty road freckled with sunlight.

He holds the reins while Prince, his white horse,
gazes across the softly hissing meadow.

In Prayers

After Mom's funeral memories arrived three on a mule.
Jansen's History of Art on the leather-topped coffee table.
Her water color of snap dragons on the kitchen window sill.
A kettle of Manhattan clam chowder simmering.

Her voice urging joy at first light on a Sunday—
"Awake for morning in the bowl of night
has flung the stone that puts the stars to flight."

I remembered coming home frozen from sledding.
They closed off the hill on 24th Street
when the big snow closed the schools.

She ran a hot bath in the old clawfoot tub
and brought me a hot mug of beef consommé.
I covered myself with a washcloth.
It was warming and delicious.

Her soothing fingers scratched my back
when I couldn't sleep
after our dog died.

She took me fishing when I was a kid.
I don't remember if I caught any,
but it stuck with me. I never told her that.

Kids don't tell their parents those things that meant something,
those things that rarely happened, maybe just once.
They don't tell them thanks until it's too late.
Then they tell them. In prayers.

Cemetery in Towamencin

When the last one
who remembers you is gone,
it's over.
On yellowed pages, I find the names,
Caspar, Balthasar, Melchior,
my Schwenkfelder forebears who fled Silesia
in wooden ships
to escape persecution
and burial in unconsecrated ground.
Melchior who became Charles in America,
in white shirt and vest, wool trousers, bunched at the knee.
In their pasture he stands beside Lydia
who sits on a ladderback chair,
gauze cap over her pinned hair,
pale hands like small birds,
folded on her apron.
In this small Pennsylvania village
Charles worked his field, while
Lydia made a garden, raised chickens,
and nine children.
Some died.
They were displayed by the altar rail
beneath satin coverlets in diminutive coffins.
Buggies hitched to the post outside waited
to carry them to sacred ground.
In a cemetery in Towamencin,
I stand before their gravestones,
worn as the slate doorsill
in their native land,
buried here and nearly forgotten.

Lydia's Sampler

His blunt fingers hold the remains of Lydia's sampler,
now just a few threads where moths had laid their eggs.

He fishes a chipped photo from his breast pocket,
a picture of his father in a dark suit, trousers creased and cuffed,

and two old ladies, barrel shaped, one standing stiffly,
dark ominous dress and those godawful shoes.

The other stares off through rimless glasses,
a black ribbon tied under her pale chin
holds her gauze cap in place.

A light powder dusts her neck,
gives off a cloying smell
that imprints in my child's memory
when she leans into him.

Midwinter

The final waters of January
spill into cold February.

In the dark,
I tap my Tibetan bells,
awaken my slumbering spirit,

light the votive candle
that waits on its dish surrounded by
white pebbles and small shells.

With palms pressed together
I whisper that I am here,
remember my mother died long ago,
longer than you think.

My father also.
I thank them for protection.

Rituals open as spirals of smoke scent the air.

There will be snow tonight,
and in the morning,
rain, cold on the window glass.

There will be the sound of the train whistle
south of Franklin Street, wistful
even as it was in my childhood.

In the Dream I See Franklin Street,

tall trees and polished horse chestnuts,
long orange leaves
fast to the pavement in the rain.

Children sit on the porch railing
of Lloyd's Corner Grocery,
fresh-scooped ice cream cones,
butterscotch and black raspberry.

I feel the smooth rose-scented palm
of Grandmother's hand.
She cups my cheek,
her watery voice warns,
There may be men in the alleyways,
and I picture Mr. Hile in his brown work boots
and brown overalls and his brown handkerchief
clutched in his thick fingers.

I hear the geese of autumn
overhead, calling
and know
it is never far away.

About the Author

John Ziegler is a poet and painter now living among the ponderosa pines on the mountains of northern Arizona.

Raised in Allentown, Pennsylvania, he spent a great deal of time on a small lake in the Pocono Mountains absorbing the natural world by way of daydream.

In childhood, images, aromas, and sounds are absorbed and integrated unconsciously into the depths of our being, available when we are not thinking, not chasing meaning.

www.ingramcontent.com/pod-product-compliance
Lightning Source LLC
Chambersburg PA
CBHW031421160426
43196CB00008B/1009